Animals at Night

by Joseph Appelbaum

SCHOOL PUBLISHERS

Cover, ©George McCarthy/CORBIS; p.3, ©MICHAEL GADOMSKI/Earth Scenes; p.4, ©PhotoDisc; p.5, ©Dr. Merlin D. Tuttle/Bat Conservation International/Photo Researchers, Inc.; p.6–7, ©David Hosking/Photo Researchers, Inc.; p.8, ©Keith Kent/Photo Researchers, Inc.; p.9, ©Darwin Dale/ Photo Researchers, Inc.; p.10, ©Scholastic Studio 10/Index Stock Imagery; p.11, ©Ken Reid/Taxi/ Getty Images; p.12, ©David Wrobel/Visuals Unlimited; p.13, ©Michael Durham/Visuals Unlimited; p.14, ©Charles Krebs/CORBIS.

Printed in China

ISBN 10: 0-15-350080-8
ISBN 13: 978-0-15-350080-0

Ordering Options
ISBN 10: 0-15-349938-9 (Grade 3 ELL Collection)
ISBN 13: 978-0-15-349938-8 (Grade 3 ELL Collection)
ISBN 10: 0-15-357262-0 (package of 5)
ISBN 13: 978-0-15-357262-3 (package of 5)

1 2 3 4 5 6 7 8 9 10 985 12 11 10 09 08 07 06

Many animals are nocturnal. Nocturnal animals are active at night. They sleep during the day. The dark night helps to hide them while they hunt or find food.

Bats

Bats are special animals. One reason that bats are special is that they are the only mammals that can fly. Humans are mammals, too.

Bats fly to find food at night. Some bats eat insects. Mosquitoes and fireflies are two kinds of insects that bats eat.

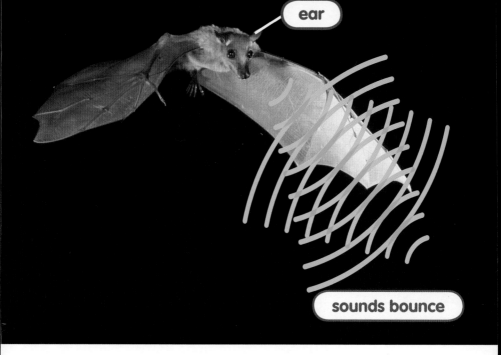

ear

sounds bounce

Another reason bats are special is that they use their ears when they hunt. How? A bat squeaks as it flies. The sounds a bat makes bounce off objects and come back to the bat. The sounds tell the bat where things are, such as food. Bats hear sounds well with their very large ears.

Owls

One kind of nocturnal bird is the owl.
Owls hunt at night. Their large eyes help
them see well in very little light. Owls fly
silently with their big wings.

Owls hunt for food. They hunt small animals, such as mice, small rabbits, and birds. Owls also eat animals such as snakes and frogs.

Fireflies ("Lightning Bugs")

Fireflies are not flies. They are a kind of beetle. They are also called "lightning bugs." Fireflies are a special part of summer. It is fun to see their golden flashes of light as they fly.

How do fireflies light up? A part of the firefly's body actually glows. Why does this happen? Each glowing flash is a signal. The signals help males and females find each other.

Baby fireflies do not fly. However, they do glow. Sometimes they are called "glowworms."

Hamsters

Hamsters are popular pets. People like them because they are cute, and they are easy pets to keep. However, as every hamster owner knows, hamsters are nocturnal. They sleep in the daytime.

Hamsters are awake at night. They nibble and dig to make nests. They run on their exercise wheels. If you like quiet at night, do not keep your pet hamster in the room where you sleep!

Catfish

Did you ever imagine that a fish could be nocturnal? Catfish are nocturnal. They eat at night. Catfish eat insects, shellfish, and other fish. The feelers on the face of a catfish help it find food. The feelers look like a cat's whiskers. That is why these fish are called "catfish."

Raccoons

Raccoons are nocturnal animals. Raccoons live in forests and in cities. They have a band of dark fur across their eyes. The band looks like a mask.

Raccoons use their front paws almost like little hands. Raccoons eat shellfish, insects, frogs, berries, and nuts. Raccoons also enjoy meals from any trash can!

All of these animals sleep during the day, but they are very busy all night long! When it is time for you to go to sleep, these animals are just getting started!

Scaffolded Language Development

PREPOSITIONS Remind students that a preposition is a word that may link a noun or a pronoun to another word. Model some placement prepositions for students by placing a book *on*, then *off*, and then *in* your desk. Then give the book *to* a student. Have students do the same with a book of their own. Read the sentences below and have students chorally fill in the blanks with the prepositions from the word bank.

Word Bank: at, in, to, off

1. Nocturnal animals hunt _____ night.
2. Raccoons can live _____ forests or cities.
3. Bats make sounds that bounce _____ objects and come back to the bat.
4. Fireflies send signals _____ other fireflies.

Science

Make a Drawing Have students make a drawing of a nighttime scene. Tell them to include animals from the book and label each animal with its name.

School-Home Connection

What Have You Seen? Have students talk to family members about times that they have seen different types of nocturnal animals. What were the animals doing when they were spotted?

Word Count: 479 (482)